# WHY DO I NEED A PERSONAL INJURY LAWYER FOR MY ACCIDENT CLAIM?

Charles P. Ward, Esq.

Ward & Ward Law Firm
728 S Meridian St
Indianapolis, IN 46225
www.WardLawFirm.com

Or email: cpw@WardLawFirm.com

Ordering Information:

Quantity sales – Special discounts are available on quantity purchases by corporations, associations, and others. For details, contact the author at the address above.

Orders by U.S. trade bookstores and wholesalers. Please contact
Ward & Ward Law Firm: Tel: (888) 639-9501 or email:

cpw@WardLawFirm.com.

Printed in the United States of America.

Published in 2018.

ISBN: 978-1-946481-29-0

# FOREWORD

If you are reading this book, you may have already been involved in an accident. My hope is that you, the reader, will understand why representing oneself in a legal claim for injuries is fraught with peril and that the only good solution to the question, *'Why do I need a personal injury lawyer?'* is because *'You don't know, what you don't know!'*

This book does not provide legal advice and it is not a substitution for hiring an attorney experienced in personal injury claims to represent you and your best interests. *(See full Disclaimer on page 8)* Every case has it's own facts and circumstances and each case turns on its own wheels. But the following pages may assist you in the selection of a personal injury lawyer and with a little luck may touch on some of the questions you have about personal injury law including payment of medical bills and insurance coverage–your safety net as you go about your daily life.

When injuries are incurred in an accident caused by the negligence of another person or entity, I have a series of guidelines I recommend following–if you are in a position to do so. I keep these posted at our website, WardLawFirm.com. By following the procedures listed below, the probability that you and your attorney will experience a successful and positive outcome in your legal claim for damages is significantly increased.

1. **Call 911 –** Request an officer be dispatched to the scene. The investigating officer will interview drivers, witnesses and assess fault based on testimony and the physical evidence. Once the officer's drawing has been incorporated into the crash report, you may request a copy. It is important to note that accidents involving death or dismemberment may delay the release of the accident report as further evidence is compiled.
2. **Request an ambulance or seek immediate medical attention –** Due to the release of a powerful hormone called adrenaline, certain injuries may go unnoticed immediately following an accident. Within a few hours or overnight the adrenaline-induced euphoric feeling of strength and well-being gradually dissipates and the pain accompanying the injuries may become symptomatic. Being seen by a medical physician immediately following an accident fulfills *your duty to*

*mitigate damages* and reduces the possibility of further damage to the injury.

3. **Get driver & witness information but do not discuss fault!** – When liability is in question, your attorney may wish to personally interview the eyewitnesses.
4. **Take photos** - Over time memories fade but photos preserve many details of the accident scene and aid the work of an accident reconstructionist if one is employed. In situations where a fatality has occurred, responding law enforcement usually sends an experienced photographer to the scene.
5. **Do not post information or photos on your social media accounts** – Since the courts have ruled there is no expectation of privacy on social media, defense attorneys may request information related to your accounts during the discovery process. Examples of social media accounts include, but are not limited to Facebook, Twitter, Instagram, Reddit, etcetera. If you have any questions about your social media accounts, talk with your attorney.

# DEDICATION

I would like to dedicate this book to the many plaintiff personal injury trial lawyers I know and have known, who have devoted their professional lives – heart and soul – to the noble pursuit of advocating for individuals who have been wronged and in need of competent legal representation – especially my father, Donald W. Ward, who has practiced in the area of personal injury law for more than six decades.

# Disclaimer

This publication is intended to be used for educational purposes only. No legal advice is being given, and no attorney-client relationship is intended to be created by reading this material. The author assumes no liability for any errors or omissions or for how this book or its contents are used or interpreted or for any consequences resulting directly or indirectly from the use of this book. For legal or any other advice, please consult an experienced personal injury attorney or the appropriate expert.

**Ward & Ward Law Firm**
728 S Meridian St
Indianapolis, IN 46225
(317) 639-9501
www.WardLawFirm.com

# TESTIMONIALS

*(These and additional reviews may be found on Google.)*

*"Eleven years ago, we lost my dad in a horrible auto accident. I will be forever grateful to a family friend of ours, (name removed for privacy), who encouraged us to contact Charlie Ward. Charlie represented her in a wrongful death case when she lost her mother in an accident as well. Charlie worked countless hours on our case and so closely with our family in order to represent us the best way he possibly could. Charlie not only cared about our case, but also about our emotions and grief in losing dad. He found a wonderful balance in fighting for us while also respecting how difficult it all was. There was never a time that we couldn't contact Charlie and that he wouldn't drop everything to talk to us. Charlie is a family man who is fair and just. I never knew you could become lifelong friends with your attorney but that is the relationship we share. I thank God that He brought Charlie into our lives during some of the most difficult days....to fight for us when we couldn't even fight."*

***- A client (name removed for privacy)***

***************

*"A few years back I was involved in an auto accident in Indianapolis, Indiana. I sustained personal injuries in the accident. Upon hearing of my situation, a friend of mine suggested that I contact personal injury attorney Charlie Ward in Indianapolis. I was very pleased with the results and would recommend him to others. It was the best decision I've ever made."*

***- A client (name removed for privacy)***

***************

*"When my daughter was three, she was bitten by a dog. We were new to the Indianapolis area, and I did not know which personal injury law firm to contact for my case. I contacted one of the large law firms in Indianapolis, and due to a conflict, they were unable to help me. However, the attorney then recommended and referred me to Charlie Ward at Ward & Ward Law Firm. I was so grateful for the recommendation. Charlie guided us through the entire process of filing a claim with the dog owner's insurance; took photographs of the injuries; and actually, listened to me when I said that the insurance company's offer was too low. We then went before a judge, explained the reason I felt my daughter should be entitled to a higher award for damages, and it was granted. Charlie, handling my case, made it much easier to deal with my daughter's injuries, and not having to worry about the claim."*

***- A client (name removed for privacy)***

***************

*"My husband,* ***(client's name removed for privacy)****, was struck and received multiple life-threatening and catastrophic personal injuries back in 2012. We had the opportunity to work with a wonderful attorney, Charlie Ward of Ward & Ward Law Firm in Indianapolis, Indiana. Charlie was available to us at any time, night or day, and helped us out during this difficult and troubling time during my husband's long period of rehabilitation. With patience and hard work, we were able to settle the claim and put it behind us. I would like to thank Charlie for his help and all that he was able to do for* ***(client's name removed for privacy)*** *and me."*

***- A client (name removed for privacy)***

***************

# ABOUT THE AUTHOR

Charles P. Ward, also known as Charlie Ward, has practiced personal injury and wrongful death law in Indianapolis, Indiana since 1994 when he and his father, Donald W. Ward, a well-known and respected Indiana attorney, jointly opened the doors to their plaintiffs' personal injury firm, Ward & Ward Law Firm. Together, father and son have combined their legal experience and talents to give voice to individuals who have been injured by the negligence of another person or entity. Collectively, Charlie and Don have acquired more than 93 years of plaintiffs' personal injury legal experience.

For nearly three decades, experienced trial lawyer Charlie Ward has served people who have been injured in the state of Indiana by negotiating, mediating and taking their claims to trial. His practice is limited to plaintiffs' personal injury cases, wrongful death claims and medical malpractice cases. Personal injury claims include, but are not limited to car accidents, motorcycle accidents, bicycle accidents, trucking and semi tractor-trailer accidents, pedestrian accidents, construction accidents, railroad accidents, aviation accidents, nursing home injury, product liability claims, dog bite injuries, slip, trip & fall injuries, medical malpractice and wrongful death cases.

Ward & Ward Law Firm has represented plaintiffs in a number of compelling and high-profile cases recovering substantial awards for their injured clients and family members of wrongful death victims. But you won't read about their clients or their compensation awards or settlements in this book or on our website at **WardLawFirm.com** because Charlie and Don Ward firmly believe that the privacy of their clients should trump any boasting of legal wins – a marketing strategy employed by some law firms to buoy their credibility. Furthermore, most large settlement agreements are contingent upon a steadfast compliance of the confidentiality clause by all parties involved; the attorneys and staff of Ward & Ward Law Firm take the oath of client confidentiality seriously.

*"We help people from all walks of life,*
*protecting the* ***Known*** *and the* ***Unknown****."*

*Charlie Ward*

# TABLE OF CONTENTS

Foreword ........ 3

Dedication ........ 6

Disclaimer ........ 7

Testimonials ........ 8

About The Author ........ 10

**Hiring An Attorney Advocate ........ 16**

Can Any Attorney Handle My Claim? ........ 16

I Have a Friend Who is a Lawyer ........ 18

Why Choose Ward & Ward to Represent You? ........ 19

No Obligation Consultation ........ 23

**What You Should Know ........ 24**

After an Accident ........ 24

Notifying Your Insurance Company ........ 25

What is a Plaintiffs' Personal Injury Lawyer? ........ 26

Can I Settle My Own Injury Claim? ........ 26

Can I Afford An Attorney? ........ 29

Qualities to Look For in an Attorney ........ 29

The Attorney Consultation ........ 31

The Attorney / Client Contract ........ 31

Witnesses and Evidence ........ 33

The Perils of Social Media ........ 34

Mistakes People Make ........ 35

Indiana's Statute of Limitations ........ 35

Rights of Passengers........................................................ 36
How Long Does it Take to Resolve a Case?.................. 38
**Do I Have a Claim for Damages? ....................................... 40**
Components of a Viable Claim....................................... 40
Do I Have a Claim If I Was Partly at Fault?.................. 41
Defenses Used to Avoid Paying Out Claims................ 42
Hit-And-Run Accidents.................................................. 43
**The Value of Your Claim .................................................... 45**
Types of Damages ........................................................... 45
Economic Damages ......................................................... 46
Non-Economic Damages ................................................. 48
Punitive Damages............................................................ 49
What is Collectability? .................................................... 51
How Is The Value Of A Claim Determined?................ 51
**Medical Treatment and Bills ............................................. 53**
Am I Obligated to Treat With a Physician?.................. 53
Early Diagnosis and Consistent Treatment .................. 54
Follow the Treatment Plan.............................................. 55
Gap in Care And Its Impact on a Claim ........................ 55
Mitigation of Damages .................................................... 56
Keeping a Journal ............................................................ 57
Should I Pay My Medical Bills?....................................... 58
Will the At-Fault Driver Pay My Bills?.......................... 59
Reimbursement of Medical Bills ................................... 59
**Medical Payment Insurance .............................................. 60**

What is Medical Payment Insurance? .......................... 60
Distribution of Med-Pay Funds.................................... 61
**Uninsured/Underinsured Motorist Coverage ................. 62**
Uninsured/Underinsured Defined.............................. 62
Is Uninsured /Underinsured Required?....................... 63
Waiving UIM Coverage................................................ 63
When Your Insurance Comes Into Play ....................... 64
Recouping Losses From An Uninsured Person ........... 65
**Understanding Automobile Insurance............................ 66**
Insurance: An Investment for Your Future................... 66
Types of Automobile Insurance Coverages.................. 67
Auto Insurance Requirements in Indiana..................... 68
Uninsured and Underinsured Coverage....................... 69
Waiving Uninsured/Underinsured Coverage............. 69
How Much Insurance is Enough?................................. 70
Insurance Recommendations........................................ 72
The Umbrella Policy– A Masterpiece!........................... 72
How Much Med Pay Insurance Should I Buy?............ 74
Do Auto Policies Cover Motorcycles? ........................... 74
Internet App-Based Rideshare Coverage...................... 75

Index ........................................................................ 77

# Chapter 1
## Hiring An Attorney Advocate

*Can Any Attorney Handle My Claim?*

I always advise potential clients to hire an attorney who limits his or her practice to personal injury law. Like physicians, lawyers *too* develop proficiency in their chosen fields. When facing the fallout of wrongs committed in a nursing home, a vehicular accident or a medical setting, it just makes sense to hire *EXPERIENCE* and maximize the value of your claim. A plethora of ever-changing state and federal laws and rulings make it impossible for any attorney to be competent in ***all*** arenas of the law. The following are some of the ever-changing factors your injury advocate should have an up-to-date knowledge of:

Judicial Decisions - Members of the Indiana State Supreme Court judiciary write opinions during every session that affect changes to tort law, medical malpractice claims, liens, etcetera. Your injury attorney should be knowledgeable about these rulings and the case law that can affect your compensation.

He waited for the next wave of regulations to arrive.

Legislation - New and amended laws and legislation that may affect your claim are created during each legislative session. [1]The Indiana Trial Lawyers Association (ITLA) is a lobby that protects the civil justice system in Indiana by advancing the interests of all citizens, injured persons and the attorneys that represent them. In 1978, my father and law partner, personal injury trial lawyer Donald W. Ward, assumed the presidency of ITLA. Today, experienced injury attorneys from all over the state

---

[1] Looking Back on the Last Fifty Years: A History of the Indiana Trial Lawyers Association. https://www.indianatriallawyers.org/index.cfm?pg=historyofitla

support ITLA because ITLA's LAW-PAC gives injured persons and grieving families a voice in the Indiana General Assembly.

## *I Have a Friend Who is a Lawyer*

It is natural to want to put your faith and financial wellbeing in the hands of someone you already know. But would you seek the assistance of a tax lawyer to represent you in a trucking accident case?

The reputation of your injury attorney has a significant bearing on the success of your case. Familiarity with personal injury law is what the insurance company is looking at. They do their research and they know the history of the attorneys representing the plaintiff; their legal team identifies which lawyers are proficient in injury law and who is a skilled and honorable negotiator. Their lawyers proceed with that information.

*Why Choose Ward & Ward to Represent You?*

Don't play musical chairs with attorney candidates. Find a lawyer that you can work well with and someone who will work hard for you. After all, a successful conclusion of your case hinges on an effective team effort.

"Since your job credentials are identical, we'll play musical chairs."

At Ward & Ward Law Firm we take pride in the work we do on behalf of our clients. The following attributes are just a few of the reasons we hope you will consider consulting with us about your claim.

Experience – The number one thing that sets our firm apart is more than nine decades of combined professional experience. We use that experience to strategize and maximize our client's monetary recovery. We know what the court requires, and we anticipate what must be proven in every case. We perform a factual investigation to minimize or exclude any type of comparative fault on our client's part. Of course, the insurance company and their attorneys always know their adversaries. They do their homework, just like we do our homework.

Relationships – We build relationships with our clients. I give every client my cell phone number and we are always available to them. Ours is an open-door policy and I encourage our clients to contact us with questions or concerns they may have. My business card contains my cellphone number for clients to use–*"Call me anytime"*–and they do!

Guidance – We guide our clients through the process, making sure they follow through with medical treatment, eliminating the mitigation of damages defense so it doesn't become an issue later.

Communication – We copy our clients on all important outgoing correspondence and touch base by phone frequently to keep them in the loop of communications. We are a transparent law firm because sincerity generates trust and the full team cooperation of our clients, attorneys and paralegals. We don't make empty promises just to keep clients happy. We are honest about what the issues are and tell our clients the truth—what they need to know–*not* what they want to hear.

Knowledge – Our up-to-date working knowledge of legal opinions, changes in the law, amendments and new legislation give our clients an edge because we calculate these variations into our strategy. Lawyers with injury experience are better equipped with staff members who remain cognizant of the rules of civil procedure and early developments in the field of personal injury law.

Attention to Details – We are thorough and deliberate in our approach to your claim. From day one through the conclusion, our ducks are aligned, I's are dotted, and T's are crossed. We go from the beginning until the end, making sure that everything is well-positioned.

Skilled Staff – Effective communication skills between attorneys and staff paralegals is vital to smooth operations in a law firm. Our firm is fortunate to have a staff that is not only loyal to the firm but who love the law and want the best outcomes for our clients. Our paralegals and legal assistants have been with the firm for many years and are bound by the same goals, i.e. the well-being of our clients.

Resources – We build trust and strong relationships to preserve and protect the resources required to adequately represent you and your loved ones for injuries that will affect you throughout your lifetime. We maintain a go-to panel of field experts we employ when the need arises.

Taking it to Trial – Every case has some pitfalls and each case turns on its own set of wheels. There are risks associated for both sides in taking a case to trial. I always tell our clients that we must look at what is in their best interest and I ask them if they feel they should resolve the claim or try the case. From day one, every case is prepared for the possibility that it will be tried in a court of law; we are equipped for any scenario.

Looking Ahead – Our firm's work speaks for itself. I tell clients I don't only protect the known–I also protect the unknown. What's known may be relevant, but *what's unknown is probably the most important part of every single one of our cases*. Our experience makes it possible for us to predict and plan for what may be expected down the road, medically and financially for our clients–long after their case has ended. We conduct our cases with the future of our clients in mind.

Making it Personal – It is the sincere desire of our attorneys and staff that every client feels we have lessened the burden of successfully managing their claim, so they may focus on healing their injuries and moving forward. *Your claim is personal to us*!

## *No Obligation Consultation*

I am happy to speak with you about your potential claim or the accident claim of your loved one. With enough information, I can usually evaluate your claim over the phone at no charge, and with no obligation or pressure put upon you. Please call *Ward & Ward Law Firm* and ask for me, *Charlie Ward*. You can also email me at the address provided below. I look forward to talking with you personally.


**Charlie Ward**
Personal Injury Attorney
Ward & Ward Law Firm
728 S Meridian St
Indianapolis, IN 46225
PH: (317) 639-9501
Email: CPW@WardLawFirm.com

# CHAPTER 2
# WHAT YOU SHOULD KNOW

*After an Accident*

If you have been in an accident caused by another person's negligence, the first thing you should do is make a call to the police or ask someone to help you. The responding officer(s) will write a report to be used as evidence in your claim. Your attorney will request this report once it has been released by law enforcement. This may take several days or even weeks in cases involving a wrongful death.

If possible, take photos of the vehicles involved, including the damage done to your vehicle. If you're physically able, talk with witnesses–take their names and contact information, including their address. *Do not admit fault in any conversations you have.* You must give an honest statement to the police.

Seek immediate medical treatment and talk with an injury attorney about your claim. I tell my clients to keep a journal–a chronology of events–from the date of the accident until the end of the claim. In it, note your pain levels, details of conversations with your physicians and therapists and loss of time off from your job.

## *Notifying Your Insurance Company*

Under all motor vehicle policies, it says, *"You have a duty to notify your company of any claim* ***or*** *of any potential claim."* In the state of Indiana, if you don't file what's called an SR-21, your license can be suspended.

Under your own policy coverage, there will be a clause for cooperation from your insurance company—also known as the Cooperation Clause. You have a *reasonable* amount of time in which to notify them of an accident. I recommend clients seek legal advice first; don't give a statement to *either* of the insurance companies, including the other side, without talking to your personal injury attorney first. They will need a statement, but your attorney should be present to protect your rights.

## *What is a Plaintiffs' Personal Injury Lawyer?*

A personal injury claim is a legal assertion that a person or persons are entitled to monetary compensation for physical, emotional and/or punitive damages as a result of the negligence or wrongdoing by another person, governmental or business entity. A plaintiff's personal injury lawyer represents the injured party or parties (also known as the claimant) and initiates the claim proceedings against the wrongdoer in pursuit of the maximum financial reparations made to their injured clients.

## *Can I Settle My Own Injury Claim?*

People can settle their own cases, but I don't recommend it. The biggest reason that you should hire an attorney to handle your personal injury claim is because there are so many pitfalls in the claims process that the majority of people know nothing about. People who have tried self-representation usually make mistakes, unbeknownst to them, that cost them in the long run. But on the other hand, if your claim is as simple as property damage alone, you should be able to handle that without legal representation.

Well-intentioned errors have been known to cause significant financial loss and future indebtedness for injury victims lacking representation. I frequently take phone calls from people who have painted themselves into a corner by trying to settle their own claim without a lawyer. By the time they realize mistakes have been made, it's too late for attorney intervention.

A few weeks ago I received a phone call from a person who had received serious injuries from an automobile accident caused by another driver. She believed she was engaged in good faith negotiations with the opposing insurance company, only to find out later that the claims representative had been stalling her while the statute of limitations ran out. By the time she called our office, it was too late to help her.

On the other hand, an insurance carrier may surreptitiously avoid a substantial payout by proposing a quick offer of settlement to the injured person before he or she hires legal counsel who will assess the ***true*** value of the claim.

Most people have no idea how to file a claim or how to go to court. The variables of laws are ongoing and they have changed so much, even for us! It's changing with Medicare, Medicaid reimbursement, ERISA plans and subrogation or reimbursement. For experienced personal injury lawyers, it is a challenge every day to stay current on judicial rulings and legislation that affects our clients – but that is our job!

When an individual attempts to settle his or her own claim with an insurance carrier, they are putting themselves at the mercy of the insurance company's defense attorneys, who are well-versed in the law. Keep in mind that insurance companies have a duty to their stockholders to put as much profit on the bottom line as possible. I am reminded of the adage, "He who represents himself has a fool for a client," *(Author unknown).*

## *Can I Afford An Attorney?*

In our office, all personal injury cases are taken on what's called the *contingency.* It doesn't cost you anything because we use our own resources to represent you. Our firm takes a percentage of whatever we recover plus costs, so it's our job to maximize the amount of recovery. Thus, we try to cover every angle on every case in order to maximize what our client will receive because we're entitled to a percentage of what we recover.

## *Qualities to Look For in an Attorney*

Choosing the right lawyer to handle your claim is crucial because the defense attorneys representing the insurance companies look at who the lawyers are, and they size them up. How the insurance company perceives the plaintiffs' personal injury attorney has nothing to do with the amount of advertising dollars they spend or billboard name recognition, but ***everything*** to do with their reputation among their legal peers. Below is a list of some of the questions that drive a defense attorney's perception of the plaintiff's attorney. These are the same qualities you should look at when you interview an attorney to represent you in your injury claim:

1. Is the attorney true to his or her word?
2. Is the attorney reasonable in their expectations?
3. Is the attorney looking to make a name for him or herself?
4. Is the attorney experienced and knowledgeable about personal injury law, legislation and judicial rulings pertaining to personal injury law?
5. Is the attorney meticulous in their investigation of the accident and thorough in the interview of eyewitnesses?
6. Is the attorney detailed and comprehensive in the preparation of their case?

Knowing how to proceed with every case that we have in our office is crucial, and that's what we do every single day. That's what our firm has done for decades. This year marks sixty-four years my dad has practiced personal injury law, and I've been at it for nearly three decades. We know what the pitfalls are. We know where defense counsel may exploit a weakness in your claim and we meet it head on to neutralize the threat.

*The Attorney Consultation*

Your first consultation with a lawyer is generally a friendly icebreaker. Whether you have received a referral from a friend, or found legal representation on Google, the attorney consultation is where you present the facts of the case and some information about yourself. Most consultations are free as this is where the attorney begins to size-up your claim and mentally unlock successful strategies. The attorney will consider any evidence available at this stage of the investigation including the police report, witness statements and drawings. He or she will ask you about your injuries, treatments and prognosis. Our attorneys frequently conduct consultations in the convenience of your home, hospital room or rehabilitation facility.

*The Attorney / Client Contract*

When an attorney agrees to handle your claim, you will be asked to sign a contract. The contract will state the percentage you agree to pay the attorney when your claim has concluded. In most cases this percentage will be applied to the gross amount of compensation you receive.

In addition, you will likely contract to reimburse your attorney from compensation you receive for the costs incurred in your claim. Costs might include postage, process service, copies, filing fees, expert witnesses, etcetera. I don't recommend attorney shopping for lower fees as they seldom vary between offices. When an attorney agrees to handle your case, understand that he or she is putting their time, their staff's time and the firm's financial resources at risk to maximize your compensation. In the state of Indiana your injury attorney generally assumes all the financial risk for your claim.

It is standard practice for injury attorneys to increase their percentage if your claim goes to trial; this is spelled out in your contract. This slight increase compensates the firm for attorney and staff hours spent in trial preparation and in court on your behalf.

Unlike some other states, Indiana is a not a pay-to play state. If you lose your case, you are not held responsible for the reimbursement of defendant's attorney's fees.

*Witnesses and Evidence*

Eyewitnesses are the most critical piece of evidence to any claim. Most observers are happy to testify because they know they may be helping an injured person or the family of a deceased victim just by retelling the facts of the event from their perspective. It is imperative your attorney and investigators speak with witnesses as early as possible in the investigation while memories of events are fresh.

I tell people to look for any type of videos and cameras that may be located on nearby buildings. You'd be surprised at how many banks, convenience stores and strip centers have video cameras that record accidents.

Photographs are important, because they may show skid marks, weather anomalies or problems with the roads, lanes and signs. Weather conditions are critically important, especially as the weather changes. Not too long ago, our firm hired pilots experienced in aerial photography; today we use drones and Google Maps to obtain the same road and engineering information.

Many vehicles come equipped with black boxes underneath the seats. Information obtained from black boxes detail acceleration, braking and RPM data up to five seconds before the accident. This data can be crucial to establishing speed, distance and reaction time. Often, we see a lot of distracted driving, or texting and driving—that's one area we find prevalent right now. Generally, the evidence from technology can really make or break a case.

## *The Perils of Social Media*

At this point I would like to add a word of caution about social media. Insurance companies use investigators to take candid, compromising photographs of injured claimants. Taken out of context, their photos may turn a sympathetic jury against the plaintiff.

But today, many plaintiffs do the work of the insurance company through their social media accounts. Insurance investigators use data mining software to search social media websites for evidence that may substantiate their defense. I tell clients *if you use social media, don't post anything regarding the accident*. It's no one's business. I try to persuade our clients from getting on social media, and telling everything that's happened in a particular case. That information is between us and the client. We'll present our evidence–our case–when the time dictates and not beforehand.

## *Mistakes People Make*

The biggest mistake that people can make in their personal injury claim are gaps in medical treatment and missing medical appointments. Under the law, you *(the plaintiff)* have a duty to mitigate damages. Regular visits to your primary and treating physicians, and/or medical specialist along with an honest effort to follow their prescribed treatment plan will illustrate your good faith intentions to mitigate your injuries. See Chapter 5 (*Medical Treatment and Bills*) for an in-depth discussion of medical treatment and ongoing care.

## *Indiana's Statute of Limitations*

The majority of tort claims in Indiana—auto, truck, motorcycle, bicycle and pedestrian accidents, product liability, nursing home, wrongful death and medical malpractice—have a statute of limitations of two years. This means a lawsuit must be on file with the court within 2 years from the date the plaintiff received or learned of their injuries. If you fail to file the claim within the 2-year timeframe, it is forever barred and there will be no further recourse. *Note: claims involving minors may have different limitation periods.*

When the at-fault party is a governmental agency involving police, firefighters, schools, etcetera, the statute mandates claimant's attorney must serve a Tort Claim Notice upon the governmental entity within a 180-day or 270-day time period from the date of the injuries. The difference in time frames depend upon the agencies involved. Additionally, a lawsuit must be filed with the court within 2 years from the date the plaintiff received or learned of their injuries.

## *Rights of Passengers*

What rights does the passenger of a vehicle have to sue for injuries and damages? As a passenger, if you have your seatbelt on and you didn't do anything wrong by causing problems in the car and you're not the driver, you potentially have a claim against the person who caused the accident. Even if the driver transporting the passenger is at fault, there may be a potential claim there–including coverage under the passenger's own uninsured–underinsured automobile insurance policy along with medical payment insurance benefits that may be available to you.

However, since [2]Indiana's Guest Statute may, under certain circumstances, shield the owner, driver and their insurance company from liability, it would be wise to consult with an experienced personal injury lawyer who can sort out the facts and make an informed assessment of your eligibility for financial compensation based upon the statute and case law.

An injured passenger in a motorcycle accident would have the same rights as the driver. Personally I recommend ***everyone*** wear a helmet because I know the devastation that can happen. But under Indiana law, motorcycle helmets are not considered mandatory safety gear. This applies to the passenger as well as the driver.

---

[2] Read about Indiana's Guest Statute: https://wardlawfirm.com/car-accident-2/how-does-indianas-guest-statute-affect-you-and-your-family/

*How Long Does it Take to Resolve a Case?*

This is the question on everybody's mind. We don't generally resolve our clients' claims until they are physically doing better or have been told by their doctors that further improvement may not be expected.

The injury will always dictate how long a claim is opened—if you settle a case prematurely and other injuries show up later on, there is no going back because the claim is over. This is why we wait to file the complaint with the court. Some people mend quicker; others just take longer to recover.

When our clients indicate they want to move forward with the case, we begin negotiations with the insurance company, always mindful of the two-year statute of limitations for filing the lawsuit with the court. In the window before the statute runs, and if negotiations have not successfully produced a settlement in line with the value of our client's claim, we will begin litigation proceedings as the statute of limitations grows ever near. After the plaintiff's attorney files the complaint with the court, the lawsuit may last anywhere from two years to ten years–*in rare cases.* A suit lasting ten years is *not* the norm.

Not all cases in litigation end up going to trial; a negotiated settlement may occur at any time. In most cases, prior to the trial date, an attempt is usually made to mediate the settlement. We never know just how long a case will last but claims generally get resolved when a client's medical condition is improved.

# CHAPTER 3
# DO I HAVE A CLAIM FOR DAMAGES?

*Components of a Viable Claim*

There are five legal components to a negligence case that must exist to constitute a viable personal injury claim. Your personal injury attorney must be able to prove the following elements are present in your claim:

1. That a duty of care is owed by the defendant(s) to the injured party;
2. That the duty of care has been breached by the defendant(s);

3. That there is a causal connection between the defendant's conduct and the resulting harm to the injured party;
4. That the resulting harm was a foreseeable event; and
5. That damages, or harm, resulted to the plaintiff from the defendant's conduct.

In an accident claim, *harm* takes the form of physical damage to the plaintiff and/or the plaintiff's property. Harms includes economic damages and non-economic damages, including, but not limited to a loss of wages, loss of love and affection, pain and suffering and impairment.

### *Do I Have a Claim If I Was Partly at Fault?*

You may have a claim even if you were partly at fault for the accident. The judge will instruct the jury that comparative fault is applied to all cases except for claims against a governmental entity for contributory negligence.

In a claim involving comparison of fault, a percentage of fault is assessed and assigned to each of the at-fault parties who bear responsibility for the accident. If there are two people responsible for causing the accident and the plaintiff is somewhat at fault, the jury may assess the plaintiff a percentage of fault. For example, 10%, 5% or even as little as 1% at-fault, depending upon the facts of the claim and the findings of the jury. comparative fault comes into play on every case that we have, but generally, there's minimal comparative fault, if any at all.

### *Defenses Used to Avoid Paying Out Claims*

There are two defenses that come up in nearly every claim. They are:

1. Comparative Fault - Comparative fault is the leading strategy that insurance companies use to avoid paying out on claims. This is where they assign and compare a percentage of fault among all the parties. If there's a governmental entity involved, there may be a contributory negligence.
2. Failure to Mitigate Damages - If you're in an accident, you have a duty to minimize your injuries. You must not wait to see a physician. I am steadfast that clients follow that rule and give all the information they can to

the medical staff or medical personnel with the desire to improve their injuries and minimize their damages.

Every case has some element of fault. I try to convey that to my clients, whether there's fault or not, that the other side will try to allege fault on the part of the claimant. You cannot change what happened. The facts speak for themselves. I counsel my clients to think about their own driving habits, breaking it down in their minds to explain to an insurance company how the accident happened.

Our duty is to exclude each one of those elements they may bring up. Insurance companies will never admit fault, so to our client the facts are purely the facts.

## *Hit-And-Run Accidents*

You can pursue a claim for hit and run, and it falls back on your own uninsured motorist coverage. If you don't know who the other person is, that also falls under your uninsured motorist coverage. You would have an ability to collect for your damages but for how much? That would depend upon your own insurance policy and how much coverage you have. I've used that many times in pedestrian cases and bicycle cases. I have two motorcycle cases right now where my clients were horribly injured and the person who caused the accident fled the scene. We have the uninsured motorist coverage underneath the hit and run policy of our client's insurance policy. Because we do have coverage for it, it is possible to recover.

# CHAPTER 4
# THE VALUE OF YOUR CLAIM

*Types of Damages*

Damages are the harms, (bodily injuries, wage loss, etc) that you have incurred, due to the negligence or recklessness of another person or entity. Your personal injury attorney will request monetary compensation for damages you have incurred.

My job as your lawyer is to maximize payment for your damages using my knowledge of law, legislation and judicial opinions, all of which may affect your claim. I begin by mentally organizing the strategy for increased compensation during our initial consultation. Negotiations for damages begin when you are feeling better or when your doctors can do nothing more to improve your outlook. If the parties involved are far apart in their expectations of your claim, litigation may follow.

There are many types of damages; each fall into one of three categories:

1. Economic Damages
2. Non-Economic Damages
3. Punitive Damages

Most of our claims involve compensation from economic damages and non-economic damages. Punitive damages awards demand establishment of defendant's behavior as *recklessly indifferent* in their causation of plaintiff's injuries.

### *Economic Damages*

Economic damages are reasonable and verifiable money damages for past, present and future losses. They can be measured, and a settlement negotiated by the parties. Examples of economic damages include:

Medical Expenses – Include, but are not limited to emergency transport services, emergency room, physicians, surgeries, medications, medical devices, physical therapy and rehabilitation costs. Medical expenses are verifiable with provider statements.

Wage Loss – Loss of wages are approximated using work history, wage and tax statements, state and federal returns; commission wages are usually historically averaged. Future losses are calculated using work history and formulas from life expectancy and inflationary tables. Future losses include but are not limited to loss of wages, work-related promotions, employment perks, lost bonuses, cost of re-training, loss of benefits and retirement plans. Wage losses are verifiably documented using universally accepted formulas.

Costs of Living with a Permanent Disability – The costs of living associated with a disability include but are not limited to medical devices, construction of housing, transportation costs and domestic services. Can be verified with medical records, statements, estimates and universally accepted formulas. Compensation for the actual disability itself is a non-economic damage for pain and suffering.

Property Damage - Vehicle and personal property loss. Property damage is verifiable with industry resources, receipts and estimations.

Burial Expenses - Includes but is not limited to plot, casket, cremation, and funeral home in a claim for wrongful death. Expenses are verifiable with statements.

## *Non-Economic Damages*

Non-economic damages describe a loss of quality of life and are synonymous with pain and suffering. The monetary value cannot be verified as the loss is subjective and can be experienced ***only by the injured party or parties***.

Pain and suffering damage cases require skilled negotiations or courtroom competency to maximize the settlement. Following are a few of the most common examples of non-economic damages:

**1.** Physical permanent impairment
2. Severe and chronic pain;
3. Mutilation, scars or deformity;
4. Sterility;
5. Loss of organs;
6. Death of a loved one;
7. Loss of love and affection; and
**8.** Loss of consortium.

## *Punitive Damages*

Claims for punitive damages may arise from product liability cases involving corporate entities or injury claims against defendant drunk drivers. Tort reform, a national campaign to place monetary *caps* on damages, has made inroads in certain fields of the law in the state of Indiana. [3]One such area where caps have been legislated is punitive damage awards.

[3] **IC 34-51-3-4** Maximum award of damages
Sec. 4. A punitive damage award may not be more than the greater of:
(1) three (3) times the amount of compensatory damages awarded in the action; or
(2) fifty thousand dollars ($50,000).
*As added by P.L.1-1998, SEC.47*

Monetary awards for punitive damages are used as a tool of the legal system to thwart outrageous conduct. The evidence must demonstrate that the defendant's behavior was intentionally willful, wanton or reckless using the following guidelines:

Willful Conduct - Implies intent to commit a wrongdoing which causes harm to another.

Wanton Conduct - Acting with reckless indifference and disregard to another's well-being.

Reckless Conduct - An act performed with a complete disregard of a predictable injurious outcome.

The amount of punitive damages levied against a defendant is limited by Indiana legislation in that awards may not exceed $50,000. [4]Distribution of awarded punitive damages is also restricted, i.e. the plaintiff receives no more than 25% of the award with the other 75% going to the state's Violent Crimes Victim's Compensation Fund.

---

[4]IC 34-51-3-6 in part states: (c) Upon receiving the payment described in subsection (b), the clerk of the court shall: (1) pay the person to whom punitive damages were awarded twenty-five percent (25%) of the punitive damage award; and (2) pay the remaining seventy-five percent (75%) of the punitive damage award to the treasurer of state, who shall deposit the funds into the violent crime victim's compensation fund established by IC 5-2-6.1-40.

## *What is Collectability?*

A viable claim for damages must have the collectability component. Collectability refers to the extent to which the wrongdoer (defendant) possesses the financial assets to pay a settlement or judgment levied against them. Assets may include the financial assistance from insurance, personal, business and/or real estate assets. Assets may also come from the uninsured/underinsured insurance and umbrella policy owned by the claimant.

## *How Is The Value Of A Claim Determined?*

Each case is different and turns on its own wheels. We take all the elements of damages into consideration including, but not limited to medical bills, loss of wages, pain and suffering, permanent impairment and disfigurement, along with our client's future prognosis. The largest portion of any claim is always about the permanency of the injuries. A soft tissue injury lasting 3 months, 6 months, or a year would not have the dollar value of a permanent injury, disfigurement or a cognitive brain injury–the largest elements that you can claim for damages.

Injuries can have an adverse effect on even the best of marriages. If there has been short or long-term damage to your marital union because of the accident, you may have a claim for loss of consortium.

When we medically understand the injuries and how the damages will influence the quality of life, we weigh the value of the damages against insurance limits and assets to determine the collectability of the claim.

# CHAPTER 5
## MEDICAL TREATMENT AND BILLS

### *Am I Obligated to Treat With a Physician?*

Under Indiana law there exists a legal standard of conduct called mitigation of damages. This means an injured person has a duty to make a good faith effort to reduce the extent of his or her injuries. A jury instruction for this asserts that any compensation awarded to the plaintiff may be reduced if the defendant(s) can prove that the injured party(ies) failed to make a reasonable effort to lessen or *mitigate* their injuries. How do you reduce or mitigate your injuries and minimize further bodily injury?

*Early Diagnosis and Consistent Treatment*

It is not uncommon for an accident victim to wait days or even months until the injury can no longer be ignored before seeking medical care. Common excuses for avoiding treatment may be:

1. Too busy - medical appointments are an unwelcome disruption;
2. Trivialization of the injury;
3. Self-diagnosis and treatment;
4. Financial hardship due to absence from work; and
5. Anxiety over medical bills.

A delay in diagnosis and follow-up treatment of accident-related injury(ies) significantly reduces the value of your claim. That is the reason why I strongly urge potential clients to be proactive in their pursuit of a diagnosis and to follow through on recommended testing and treatment which may be ordered by an ER physician or your primary care doctor. Such timely intervention may not only reduce the extent of injuries, but demonstrates a sincere effort to lessen the injury, minimizing further damage.

## *Follow the Treatment Plan*

While you are treating for your injuries, do not miss or cancel appointments. *This is crucial to your claim!* I tell my clients to go to the doctor, layout your problems and let the doctor address your concerns. You're only going to the doctor for one reason and that's because you have pain. If you wait too long to seek treatment, the insurance company may claim your injuries are minimal or were further aggravated by your delay in treatment. Both defenses mean a reduction in the value of your claim.

## *Gap in Care And Its Impact on a Claim*

A gap in care is a period where no treatment is being sought or rendered for an injury. For example, if you have a neck injury and you go to the doctor on the first of the month, and then wait another 30 days before you go for the second visit, that's a gap in care. *A gap in care is a huge pitfall for your claim.*

Insurance companies like to know what's happening medically. A witness or potential witness in a case, (a husband, wife, or child) can testify what mom or dad is going through, but only the medical testimony by a qualified physician carries any real weight. You don't want it to appear that you don't have ongoing or legitimate medical issues. You want to get your medical issues addressed as soon as you can because insurance companies will want to know why you prolonged getting treatment. It's hard to go back and justify your actions when you don't seek treatment. That's why gaps in treatment are always difficult. I try to make sure clients understand that consistent, ongoing treatment, from beginning to end, is essential–not only from the stance of good health, but also for your claim.

## *Mitigation of Damages*

Your medical specialist or primary care physician can testify as to what your medical conditions were, both prior to, and after the accident. When you don't follow the doctor's order, that's usually where you're failing to mitigate your damages. Remember, as a claimant (or plaintiff) to a legal claim for damages, you have a duty to minimize the harm and curb the result of someone else's negligence. The law states if you fail to reduce or minimize the damages, the court can decrease the amount of your financial recovery by a proportion equal to the amount of damages incurred because of your failure to mitigate. It's very important not to have that gap in treatment.

*Keeping a Journal*

A daily journal tells your story of pain levels, pain triggering events, and treatments as you progress through your recovery. I tell clients every day that the only way you can communicate your pain levels with your provider is to keep track of your pain in a journal. Use the numbers in Figure 1 to describe your pain levels. Keep track of conditions that produce pain and what, if anything, reduces the pain. If there is a time of day when your pain is better or worse, note that in your journal as well.

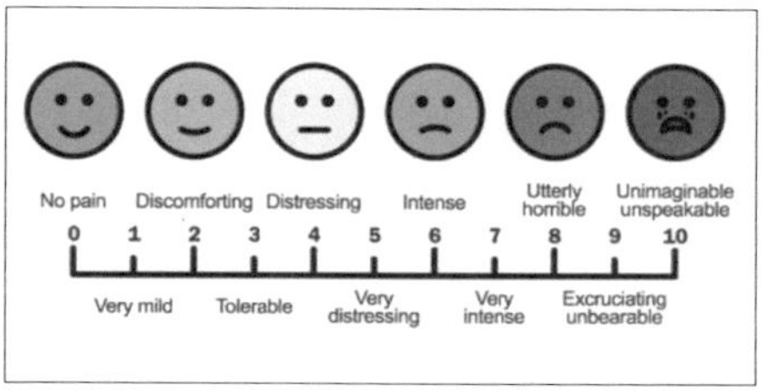


Share your pain levels with your medical providers. If you're doing better, let them know that. If you have more problems in a particular area, inform them of that also.

Keep track of tests, surgeries, injections, physical therapy sessions and medical devices, along with notes from conversations with your physicians, including suggestions and referrals. Your doctor's recommendations are the most critical to follow for evidence in your claim for damages.

### *Should I Pay My Medical Bills?*

One of the biggest elements or issues we see with people trying to handle their own claims is they don't understand how health insurance and medical payment coverage works to their benefit. I have a strategy I use in determining how medical bills are paid.

I educate my clients that we want to proceed with their own health insurance because the biggest discounts are available through medical billing. If you volunteer your automobile med-pay insurance as the primary payer to your hospital accounts representative, the limits will exhaust quickly as it is generally paid at 100% of whatever the bill is. [5]If you have ever questioned the fairness of hospital charges, read my blog about the hospital Charge Master entitled *Are You Paying Too Much for Hospital Care?*

---

[5] https://wardlawfirm.com/car-accident-2/are-you-paying-too-much-for-hospital-care/

I prefer to use medical payment insurance, also known as med-pay, as secondary insurance for paying smaller statements such as office visits, doctor fees, therapy and x-rays. This shrinks the list of outstanding providers as your case nears resolution.

### *Will the At-Fault Driver Pay My Bills?*

The at-fault driver will not pay for your medical bills up front. Compensation for the medical bills portion of your claim is always paid in settlement. See Economic Damages - Chapter 4 (*The Value of Your Claim*)

### *Reimbursement of Medical Bills*

Your health insurance will be the primary reimbursement of your medical bills. If you are on Medicare or Medicaid that would be primary. If you were in the military, your VA benefits would be primary. Another source is through your medical payment insurance coverage and your own automobile insurance policy. In some instances, a premises liability case for example, there may be medical pay benefits available that would apply to help pay the medical bills.

# CHAPTER 6
## MEDICAL PAYMENT INSURANCE

### *What is Medical Payment Insurance?*

Medical Payment insurance–also called Med-Pay coverage– *unless waived by the policyholder,* is included on your automobile or homeowner's insurance policy for medical bills associated with your claim. You pay an *inexpensive* premium for it. You may increase your policy's med-pay limits for a small charge—only *pennies on the dollar*—to get more coverage.

Example: You may pay as much as $20 for $5,000 worth of medical coverage on your automobile policy. Or you may pay $25 for $25,000 worth of coverage. It may only be another $5 for $50,000 worth of coverage. These rates are set. So again, the more you buy the cheaper it is by the unit.

### *Distribution of Med-Pay Funds*

I encourage my clients to follow a plan that will maximize their final compensation check. It's always your health insurance first, as the primary payer of any medical bills. Then you should use your medical payment coverage underneath your policy as a secondary payer to fill in the portions you are responsible for. For example, if you are billed for a service costing $5,000, (like an MRI) you would send the outstanding portion to your automobile insurance company for medical payment only ***after*** your healthcare insurance pays their portion of the bill.

Should you run out of medical-payment benefits, my staff works with your medical provider's accounting department to reduce the risk of going into collection That's why it is so important for our clients to send us the bills and any other correspondence they receive from the provider.

# CHAPTER 7
## UNINSURED/UNDERINSURED MOTORIST COVERAGE

*Uninsured/Underinsured Defined*

An uninsured motorist is a person at fault for an accident that has no insurance coverage. Technically the plaintiff (claimant) would have to look to their own company for uninsured motorist coverage. You may also see uninsured motorist coverage come into play in a hit and run accident when the driver responsible for the injuries leaves the scene of the accident.

An underinsured motorist is someone with low policy limits– insufficient insurance for the damages. Your underinsured coverage would go above and beyond the limits of the at-fault driver. For example, if they have $25,000 and you have a $100,000 worth of coverage, you may collect as much as $75,000 from your own policy, and $25,000 from the underlying carrier. Indiana though requires a minimum of $50,000 for underinsured motorist coverage, which is a good thing.

### *Is Uninsured /Underinsured Required?*

Unfortunately, uninsured/underinsured coverage should be required in Indiana, but it is not. You can actually waive this inexpensive coverage, but we don't recommend it.

### *Waiving UIM Coverage*

In Indiana, uninsured/underinsured insurance, also known as UIM, is included in every liability policy unless you specifically waive the coverage. Waiving your uninsured/underinsured coverage on your policy only saves a few pennies on the dollar–but it could cost you considerably if you need it and do not have it. Once in a while we see incidents where it is necessary to make a claim for uninsured/underinsured insurance, but prior to the accident the policyholder waived their coverage to lower their premium. Unfortunately, this may become more prevalent as folks try to reduce the cost of their policies.

I've seen liability policies where the cost for uninsured/underinsured coverage is minimal–only $5 to $10–and people waive it when the sales representative states, *you don't need this extra coverage*. The problem is too many people have no idea what they are waiving until they need it.

When you purchase your policy, ask your agent if your policy covers uninsured and underinsured claims. Then check your policy and your declarations page to be certain you have this crucial coverage and are paying for it. *Do **not** waive any type of automobile coverage!*

## *When Your Insurance Comes Into Play*

When the person who caused the accident has a minimal liability insurance policy, your attorney will proceed to collect against that person, and then file a claim with your own uninsured or underinsured motorist carrier. There are laws in place that mandate specific steps be followed and this can be tricky for people trying to settle their own claims. If the process is not performed correctly and as mandated by legislation, unknowingly, you could waive your right to the additional compensation you deserve.

I had one of those cases this week where a person tried to handle his own claim. He settled with the underlying carrier for $25,000 and signed their release, not realizing he had another $75,000 underlying coverage he could have, *and should have,* collected. By not following the proper procedures, his underlying coverage was waived.

### *Recouping Losses From An Uninsured Person*

If the other driver is uninsured, your insurance policy is your only route to compensation. I always tell my clients, *I don't care what insurance the other person has, I care about what* ***you*** *have.* I've had many clients call me after subsequent accidents to say, *Thank God, we had the coverage that we had because of what you told us.*

# CHAPTER 8
# UNDERSTANDING AUTOMOBILE INSURANCE

*Insurance: An Investment for Your Future*

I would say that 95% of our clients have no idea how much insurance coverage they have. When it becomes necessary to use their insurance, they are shocked at the lack of coverage. I always ask people if they have insurance. If they don't, I advise them to buy the best protection they can possibly afford–certainly, a policy with limits greater than the minimum required to legally drive in Indiana. After you have read the previous chapter on Uninsured/Underinsured Motorist Coverage, you will understand why I care more about ***your*** policy than the other driver's policy.

*Types of Automobile Insurance Coverages*

Automobile insurance prices are not set by the state of Indiana–but they *are* regulated. Before they may publish their prices, risk companies must submit their rates to the [6]Indiana Department of Insurance. If their rates are deemed fair and non-biased, they may be put into effect.

Take a look at the Declarations page of your automobile insurance policy. The most important coverages and the largest expenditures will be in the following categories:

<u>Bodily Injury and Property Damage</u> – Separate coverages that respectively pay out to the other driver for bodily injuries received and property damage caused by you.

<u>Medical Payment</u> – Pays medical bills incurred by you and usually your passengers, up to the limits of the policy, if injured.

---

[6] https://www.in.gov/idoi/2579.htm

Collision – After the deductible, collision insurance pays for damage to your car caused by crash or upset. *Note: the book value of a totaled vehicle may fall short of your loan balance.*

Comprehensive – After a deductible is met, comprehensive insurance pays for damages to your vehicle caused by acts other than collision or upset. Common losses include but are not limited to glass breakage and theft.

In addition, your declarations page may reflect add-on enhancements to your policy including towing and car rental coverages.

### *Auto Insurance Requirements in Indiana*

The minimum liability limits for the state of Indiana are $25,000/$50,000/$25,000. The first two numbers respectively represent $25,000 maximum liability per person, per accident, and up to $50,000 maximum per accident to be proportionally divided among a multiplicity of injured persons. Underinsured motorist liability coverage is $50,000. The last set of numbers represent $25,000 policy limits for property/vehicle damage.

### *Uninsured and Underinsured Coverage*

Your uninsured/underinsured coverage protects you, your family and friends from an act of negligence committed by uninsured and underinsured drivers, i.e. those that have little or no insurance whatsoever. Despite the implementation of legislation making it illegal to drive without insurance in the state of Indiana, there are many uninsured drivers on our roads. In 2017, the Insurance Information Institute estimated that Indiana ranks 8th in the nation for the highest number of uninsured drivers at 16.7%. Florida ranks #1 at 26.7%.

It is next to impossible to assess the number of underinsured drivers in Indiana as the term *underinsured* is *relative to the needs of the injured party(ies)*. For statistical purposes, the term *underinsured* cannot be measured.

### *Waiving Uninsured/Underinsured Coverage*

All insurance companies are required under Indiana law to offer uninsured/underinsured motorist coverage. Bur if you are willing to accept financial responsibility for injuries and damages caused by a driver without insurance, you have the right to waive your uninsured/underinsured motorist coverage. *I do not recommend waiving this coverage under any circumstances!*

### *How Much Insurance is Enough?*

A minimum risk policy is not adequate. For example, a single injured person taken by ambulance to a trauma hospital for testing, treatment, and an overnight stay may rapidly exceed the bodily injury policy limits of $25,000 per person.

I recommend you purchase the best coverage you can afford. If an uninsured driver hits you and you only have the minimum legal limits, you may be indebted for the injuries you and family members sustain for years to come. Buy your policy–not only to reduce your exposure for an accident *you* may cause–but to safeguard your family should an uninsured or underinsured driver injure you or a family member. I always ask my clients about their policy limits. Why? Because their claim may involve *their own* underinsured motorist coverage

Search Google for "Buy Indiana car insurance" to find out how many companies use "Cheap," "Very cheap" and "Cheap state minimum" in their advertising snippets. These phrases dominate the pages! Insurance companies actively market the cheapest, legal insurance policies available–not the kind of policies that protect families and livelihoods. They routinely offer quotes for the lower-limit policies because the company potentially suffers less risk.

[7]Ask your insurance representative to quote a $250,000/$500,000 policy and you will find that the additional coverage may cost you only pennies a day more than the base minimum. In fact, insurance actually becomes cheaper by the unit (per $1,000) as the number of units purchased increase. This is generally true for all liability and medical payment policies as they climb in value.

---

[7] See the results of our test quotes for various insurance policies at: https://wardlawfirm.com/bicycle-accident/increase-your-liability-insurance-coverage-for-personal-protection-against-auto-motorcycle-bicycle-pedestrian-and-trucking-or-semi-tractor-trailer-accident-claims/

*Insurance Recommendations*

Most injury attorneys would concede that minimum limits are inadequate. Personally, and professionally, I recommend everyone have a minimum of $250,000-$500,000 coverage with an added umbrella policy. The umbrella is a general protection both ways—whether you cause the accident, or someone else causes the accident. *Do not waive the uninsured/underinsured coverage of the umbrella policy.*

*The Umbrella Policy – A Masterpiece!*

An umbrella policy is also called an Excess Policy. If the damages exceed the underlying auto insurance of $250,000, the question is *can you collect?*

When the other person has no insurance or assets, you have to look at what you have in the way of coverage. Example: Theoretically, the at-fault driver has $250,000 of coverage – or *you*, through your uninsured/underinsured policy, may have $250,000 for the coverage. If you carry an umbrella policy, the damages that are above that are what they consider *excess* – above and beyond your policy or the other person's policy benefits. I'll give you another example.

If the at-fault driver has $25,000 in auto insurance–and it's a horrible injury case–and you have $250,000 in automobile coverage with an umbrella that has uninsured/underinsured motorist coverage, you first collect $25,000 from the at-fault party's underlying carrier. If the damages warrant, you may collect an additional $225,000 from your own underlying auto carrier because your auto insurance company gets what's called the *'setoff'* under Indiana law. This means that whatever amount the other insurance company pays gets subtracted from your coverage.

Then the combined damages that go above and beyond the $250,000 is what goes into the umbrella. So, if you have a million-dollar umbrella policy and you're horribly injured, you potentially may collect another million dollars beneath your umbrella policy.

Most people that have insurance don't know about umbrellas. I try to educate all of our clients to purchase an umbrella policy because as of 2017, it costs about $500 a year for that $1 million dollars of coverage and your peace of mind.

*How Much Med Pay Insurance Should I Buy?*

A trip to the hospital, may cost $5000 – $10,000 for just an ambulance ride. When you factor in the ER visit, x-rays, bloodwork, MRI and other hospital charges, I tell clients that $25,000 of medical payment insurance is an absolute minimum.

The more med-pay insurance you buy, the cheaper it becomes. In today's world, $5,000–$10,000 of med-pay reimbursement is just not going to cut it. You need $25,000 at a minimum, just to get the process going. Those funds would be used in combination with the benefit of your primary health insurance to maximize your benefits.

*Do Auto Policies Cover Motorcycles?*

Generally, Motorcycle risk is excluded under your automobile insurance policy. If you don't own a separate policy for your motorcycle, then you don't have the coverage.

*Internet App-Based Rideshare Coverage*

Transportation Network Companies (TNC), offer internet *(usually app-based)* ridesharing services that connect passengers with drivers for monetary compensation. Unlike medallion taxi companies, almost anyone can become a driver for a TNC.

For the most part, TNCs require their driver-partners to purchase an auto policy that will cover ride-shares. As of this writing, one such company offers a supplemental policy, but only when the app is turned on before the ride is requested. Most insurance companies have excluded ridesharing from their auto policies including coverages such as personal injury protection, medical payment protection and uninsured/underinsured coverages. Check your policy exclusions before contracting for a ride.

If it is your intention to work within a transportation network platform that does not provide insurance for their contractors, inquire with your underwriter about a separate policy.

If you use internet-based ride-sharing services, research how much liability insurance the TNC and/or the driver carry before you accept a lift to your destination. If your automobile insurance underwriter has excluded transportation network platforms (TNP) from your own policy, your insurance will not cover you for liability, medical payment and uninsured/underinsured protections.

# INDEX


### *A*

ACCIDENT CLAIM · *23, 41*

AUTOMOBILE INSURANCE · *67*

### *B*

BICYCLE · *11, 35, 44, 71*

BODILY INJURIES · *45, 67*

### *C*

CHEAP STATE MINIMUM · *71*

CLAIMANT · *26, 36, 43, 51, 56, 62*

COLLECTABILITY · *51, 52*

COLLISION INSURANCE · *68*

COMPARATIVE FAULT · *19, 41, 42*

COMPARISON OF FAULT · *See* Comparative Fault

COMPENSATION · *11, 17, 26, 31, 32, 37, 45, 46, 50, 53, 61, 65, 75*

COMPREHENSIVE INSURANCE · *68*

CONSULTATION · *31, 46*

CONTINGENCY · *29*

CONTRACT · *31*

CONTRIBUTORY NEGLIGENCE · 42

COOPERATION CLAUSE · *25*

### *D*

DISABILITY · *47*

DISCLAIMER · *3, 7*

### *E*

ECONOMIC DAMAGES · *41, 46*

ERISA PLANS · *28*

EVIDENCE · *4, 24, 31, 33, 34, 50, 58*

EXCESS POLICY · *72*

### *F*

FAULT · *4, 5, 25, 36, 37, 41, 42, 43, 59, 62, 63, 72, 73*

### *G*

GAP IN CARE · *35, 55*

GUEST STATUTE · *37*

### *H*

HELMET · *37*

HIT AND RUN · *43, 62*

### *J*

JUDICIAL OPINIONS · *45*

## L

LEGISLATION · *17, 21, 28, 30, 45, 50, 65, 69*
LIABILITY INSURANCE · 76
LITIGATION · *38, 39, 46*
LOSS OF CONSORTIUM · *52*
LOSS OF WAGES · *47*

## M

MEDICAID · *28, 59*
MEDICAL BILLS · *3, 51, 54, 58, 59, 60, 61, 67*
MEDICAL EXPENSES · *47*
MEDICAL MALPRACTICE · *11, 17, 35*
MEDICAL PAYMENT INSURANCE · *37, 59, 74*
MEDICAL TREATMENT · *20, 25*
MEDICARE · *28, 59*
MINIMUM LIABILITY LIMITS · *68*
MITIGATION OF DAMAGES · *20, 53, 56*
MONETARY RECOVERY · *See* COMPENSATION
MOTORCYCLE · *11, 35, 37, 44, 71, 74*

## N

NEGLIGENCE CASE · 40
NON-ECONOMIC DAMAGES · *41, 46, 48*

## O

OPINIONS · *17, 21*

## P

PASSENGER · *36, 37*
PAY-TO-PLAY · *32*
PEDESTRIAN · *11, 35, 44, 71*
PERSONAL INJURY CLAIM · 26, *27, 35, 40*
PERSONAL INJURY LAW · *3, 6, 9,* 16, *18, 30*
PERSONAL INJURY LAWYER · *3, 26, 37*
PLAINTIFF · 36
POLICY EXCLUSIONS · *75*
PROPERTY DAMAGE · *27, 48, 67*
PUNITIVE DAMAGES · *26, 46, 49, 50*

## R

REIMBURSEMENT · *28, 32, 59, 74*
RIDESHARING SERVICES · *75*
RULINGS · *16, 17, 28, 30*

## S

SELF-REPRESENTATION · *27*
SETTLEMENT · *12, 28, 38, 39, 46, 48, 51, 59*
SOCIAL MEDIA · *5, 34*
SR-21 · *25*

STATEMENT TO INSURANCE COMPANY · *26*

STATUTE OF LIMITATIONS · 27, 35

### *T*

TEXTING · *34*

TORT CLAIM NOTICE · *36*

TRIAL · *6, 11, 17, 22, 32, 39*

### *U*

UMBRELLA POLICY · *51, 72, 73*

UNDERINSURED · *37, 62, 63, 64, 68, 69, 70*

UNINSURED MOTORIST COVERAGE · 43

UNINSURED/UNDERINSURED · *51, 63, 64, 69, 72, 73, 75, 76*

### *V*

VA BENEFITS · *59*

### *W*

WITNESSES · *4, 25, 32, 33*

WRONGFUL DEATH · *8, 10, 11, 24, 35, 48*

# NOTES

Made in the USA
Monee, IL
05 November 2026

67385065R00050